To:

From:

You Stink!
I love you
From brothers and sisters, of course

Compiled and Illustrated by Stuart Hample

WORKMAN PUBLISHING • NEW YORK

Cataloging and publication information is available from the Library of Congress.

Workman books are available at special discounts when purchased in bulk for premiums and sales promotions as well as for fund-raising or educational use. Special editions or book excerpts can also be created to specification. For details, contact the Special Sales Director at the address below.

Special thanks to Mrs.Coveler's class at The Village School, Ms.Shannon's class at Thomas J. Leahy Elementary School and Mrs.Day's class at Greenwood Country Day School

Cover and interior design by Lisa Hollander and Susan Macleod

Workman Publishing Company, Inc.
708 Broadway
New York, NY 10003-9555
www.workman.com

Printed in the United States of America

First printing: March 2002
10 9 8 7 6 5 4 3 2 1

BUT FOR WHOM

One day my son Zack said,
"Hey, Pop, you should do a book about
siblings." Thanks to him, here it is.

Thanks also to Joanne Sherman of the *Shelter Island Reporter*; to Joe La Rosa for extensive favors; to educators Joyce Blyn, Terry Costin, Kim Westfall, Carla McElroy, Gilbert di Cicco, Sharon Kilb Gibbs, Jennifer Rylott, Cheryl Woods, Steve Plaut, Dana Hart, Michelle Yang, Rita De Brito, Stanley Seidman, Sue Longenecker, Meryl Blumenthal, Evyan Lieberman, Cynthia Chait, Ryan Flessner, Marcelle Roe Langendahl, Letisha Ellis, Jesse Pasca, Rachel McGoldrick; and to the kids who wrote about their sibs.

CONTENTS

INTRODUCTION

The testimonies that follow (with lapses in spelling and grammar untouched) come from the child's land of siblings, where the currency is Truth. Euphemisms and equivocations do not exist. Only the extremes of disdain or adoration matter—often simultaneously.

But while accusations of mistreatment are pervasive (the words *annoying* and *mean* pop up often), what comes through is a sense of alliance. These adversaries (ages 7 to 13) are, in the final analysis, bound not so much by bickering as by blood; the reports they file from the front are full of joy and devotion. What better definition could there be for that special place where only brothers and sisters live?

— Stuart Hample

Annoyances,

Petty & Otherwise

My sister Jenny
thinks she's God.
Boy is she wrong!

Alison

Jonathan A. is a
psycho.

Moira A.

My dad said when my
little brother bugs me
I have to anser with
words not hitting. But
it's hard so some times I
do both of them

Natasha

Me and my sister Denise,
it's not exactly hate,
it's more like competition.

Ruby

My sister doesn't even weigh that much but anyway everything she eats she tells you how many calories are in it as if you really care

Craig

Sometimes I and my sister get along. But when we do it is usually because my mom makes us.

Neal

My sister's 14. Once I just said "Hi" and she yells

LEAVE ME ALONE ! ! ! !

Louisa

I have two brothers and I
am in the middle. I am
very outnumbered. Except for
my Mom because even my cat
is a boy.

Erika

My sister is 1½.
She likes when
I feed her, but
when she doesn't
like the food,
She spits it in my face.

Natalie G.

Me and my brother were doing the laundry then he took the elevator up to our apartment and pressed every button except basement. So I had to wait 10 minutes until the elevator came back down. He is definitely not a perfect brother.

Isac

Sometimes if I'm alone I kneel
down on my knees and say:
"God, I would love to have
a sister I could share lots
of things and lots of secrets
with." Unfortunately, I have
a brother.

By Ellie

My sister is a spoiled brat. I could say I love her but that would be a lie.

Lelia

What we need in our family
to keep us from getting on
each others nerves is about
three more computers.

Frances

My brother thinks he's
ghetto. He wears his pants
all the way down and he just
thinks he's so cool. But he's
really a dork.

Jordan

I think my sister
bugs me because
I bug her, but it's
sort of hard not to
because we're sisters.

Laura

I have a brother who is 2 years old.

What I would like to say about him is

that he steals stuff and he bites.

Sherra

The Most annoying
Thing my brother does
is when he has a
secret. Then he
Comes and leans
over me and yells
in my ear.

Johnny

I have five sisters.
I need a brother.

Timmy

we are having a New
baby. I hope it doesn't
stay around for ever.

Mickey

My sister's 3. She'll take whatever she wants from my room and just throw it down the stairs. But then the next minute she's like, I love you, Margie. Oh sure!!!

Margaret

My brother is three years old
His name is Oscar. He was born
in Saint Mary Hospital.
But believe me he is
no saint.

Johanna

My Brother

We get a prize if we can go for a whole day with no hitting. Like they let us stay up to watch the end of the world series. And they took us two times to the ice-cream store. But those was last year.

Manuel

Observations, Doubts

& Random Information

My sister and I never get along. My parents get sick of it because the only thing they hear is "I hate you" and things like that. We know we don't mean it but they're totally clueless.

Nina

My little Brother can be sweet, but you still have to be very careful. One time he said, "Sara I'm gonna marry you." I said "Nathan, you can't marry me I'm your sister." So he kicked me.

Sara

I have two older step-brothers
and one older step-sister.
But I like them just as much
as if they were real.

Lukas

Mindy she fell in some
Poison ivy and I would of
hugged her so she'd feel
better exept I was afraid
I'd get it to.

Neila

One time me and my brother were wresling. Then my mom said "stop the nonsense and eat your supper. So, he goes "tell dumbhead to pass the bread". I go "tell dork brain I don't pass stuff to people who call me names". Then we started laughing so hard it wrecked the fight.

Leigh

Sometimes my brother's a
Jerk. and Sometimes he's nice.
He Should learn about how not
to be a Jerk, then he would
be awesome.

Ricky

My brother Ronnie is 6. He tells
everybody that he drives
our car. But he doesn't
say it's when he sits on my
father's lap.

Stefan

Christmas is when my
brothers are the best.
They give me presents
and they are not annoying.
To bad it's only one day.

Marley

when I get Married and
Have Kids i will never
PUNISH THE older one
LiKe wHeN My little
Sister Hits me and I
Hit Her back tHeN
I caNt watcH T.V.
But SHe still caN.

Ned

my dad and my mom
talk in Spanish so we
won't know what they're
saying. So me and my
sister we talk in our
secret language. Then
they don't know what
we're saying either.
Elena

I wondered what it would be like to be the only child and it came true when my brother went to college. It wasn't right at night, there was no music playing next door. It felt like I was the only living creature alive.

Alice

My Brothers and Sister

At special times me and my sister and my brothers make up funny words to famous songs. Then we sing our made up words Then everybody is happy together.

Kitty

My brother Wilford has the same name as my dad. I was the next one born and there wasn't any more names the same as them. So I only get to be Warner. It begins with a w but after that it's not as good.

Warner

Me and my brother

The best thing I like to do together with him is water ski. My dad hooks two ropes to the boat so both of us can hold on together. So then he isn't always better than me just because he's bigger.

Janine

I don't like my big brother when he splashes freezing water on my face to wake me up. When I do like him is when he pays me to clean his room.

Judi

My sister does everything with me, so sometimes I get sick of her aNd we fight a lot. But since we do everything together, it wouldn't be the same without her

Millie

~~~~~~

Tributes & Accolades

(Some with Reservations)

~~~~~~

I have a sister named Gisell.
I guess she's okay but I'm not sure because she can't talk yet.

Luis

My sister is nice and
kind to me
I am lucky to have her.
I love my sister very much.

And I'm not just saying it
because she might read this.

Urvi

My brother's 15.
He burps a lot.
He's really
  disgusting sometimes,
and he tells really
disgusting jokes.
But that's ok
  because they're
  funny.
            Emily

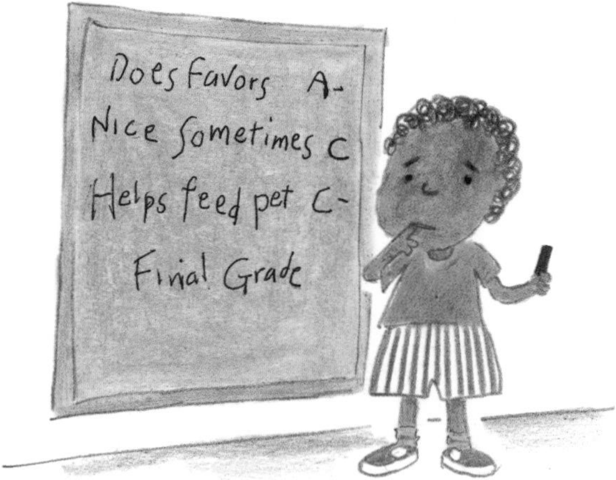
Does Favors A-
Nice Sometimes C
Helps feed pet C-
Finial Grade

My sister is almost 12 years old. sometimes we get into big fights and not just happy fights. But sometimes she helps me feed my guinea Pig. So as a sister I give her about a B+.

Jonathan

I have one sister ,11 and she's impossible but not every time. When we both were in the car and somebody had to sit in the seat that smelled like coffee which was really revolting, we fought over it and she gave in. But that's just one of about 85 million.

Nila

My sister is 3. I like that she's not old enough to tell on me if I watch TV when I'm supposed to be doing my homework.

Edward

My brother Nate is 8 months old. He can't do anything. He's just learning how to crawl. He can talk but not real talk. But he's fun to play with because he's like a toy only human.

Melody

I like my brother alot. He's 13.
I like that he stands up for me.
When his friends comment about
a stupid thing I'm doing, he says
"Shut up Dude, she's my sister."

Megan

My sister Sasha is 17
She has Bleached White
hair and a nose ring. When
my parents are out and she's
baBy sitting she always lets
me STAY UP Late and eat Junk.

tessa

Me and my 3 year old sister have bunk beds. She always comes up and sleeps with me. It's fun except when she brings up all her stuffed animals. Then there's no room left.

Fay

what I like about my
sister is that I'm
bigger than her.
ETHAN

I'm glad to have a big brother. One day when I was eight I was crying because my finger got cut and my brother fell on purpose and it was very, very funny so I would feel better.

Chandi

The best part about my sister
is teasing her about her Boy
friends. Her Boy friends are a
dumb kid in camp named
Miles, and pukey Seth.

Jared

When my sister comes home from college it's kind of weird, because I've been living there the whole year, then she just totally takes over. And that's probably the only thing I maybe don't like about her.

Gaby

I got a sister who is 16 years old.
I like her smile and the color of her
hair and how it shines in the sun.
And also I have another sister
Katie and when I tickle her tummy
she stars laughing and
I love them so much I can't
even count up that many.

Chelsea

Me and my sister Cathrine!!!

My sister makes me nuts verry!!!
When I try to sleep she wakes me
up. And she always bothers me..
But I know when we grow up we
will be best friends.

Molly

An Essay On My Brother

For a younger brother he's very mature. I'm not one of those kids that they hate their brother. If he didn't exist I would feel sad because having him makes me feel happy and not alone.

Stephen

Once I leaned too far over on a dock and fell in the water! My brother got really scared! Now when he says he hates me, I know he really cares about me deep down and that makes me feel better.

Francine

I like my older brother because
(even though this kind of sounds
like something you wouldn't
want someone to do) he picks
me up, throws me around, and
drops me on the floor. But it's
so fun and I really like it.

Nicholas

What I like about
Fabricio is that he is part
of my family.

Javier